This book belongs to:

_____

Dedicated To:

Jynx, Spaz & Kyle

Cane's sister and brothers who cared for Daddy Scott before he
was adopted.
They have already crossed the Rainbow Bridge, but the memories
of their love, devotion and silliness will last forever.

Love you always,
Daddy Scott

Written by: Scott Withers
Illustrated by: Juliet Frost
Contact info: julietfrostwork@gmail.com

The Christmas Eve Blizzard

Cane and Friends Save Santa

By
Scott Withers
Meteorologist

Illustrated by
Juliet Frost

It was already getting cold outside as Cane and his daddy drove north in their red truck. They were going to visit his Grandma Cindy to celebrate Christmas. They would arrive just in time for Christmas Eve dinner and before Santa made his deliveries.

Cane was very excited to see his grandma. He also wanted to spend time with his animal friends who live in the forest behind her house.

It was a very long drive. They had been riding in the truck almost all day. As he looked out the window, Cane noticed things looked much different from where he lived. None of the trees had any leaves, and when he pressed his nose against the window, it got very cold! His daddy said that this is the time of the year called winter. Daddy's job was telling people the weather on TV. Their truck had lots of computers and tools to help his daddy know the weather.

The longer they drove, the colder it got outside. The truck's windows started to get frozen. Daddy turned up the heater to keep it warm inside the truck.

"Cane, if you breathe on the window, it will warm up the glass, and you will be able to see outside," said his daddy.

Cane took a deep breath and blew on the window. It worked! He could see again. But something strange was happening outside. He saw large white blobs falling from the sky. Cane had never seen anything like them before.

"Daddy, what is all that white stuff falling from the sky?!" Cane barked.

"That's snow," said Daddy. "During winter, it gets cold outside, and the temperature drops. Then the water in the sky freezes into snowflakes. They fall from the sky, land on the ground, and make everything look white."

The snow was very pretty to look at. Some of the snowflakes hit the truck's window.

Daddy pointed at the snowflakes. "Every snowflake is different," Daddy said. "They all have a different size and shape. That's what makes every snowflake unique and important, just like people and animals."

Cane looked out the window again and saw a lot more snow.

"Daddy, what's happening?" Cane barked. "There are so many snowflakes, it's hard to see the trees."

"We're in a snowstorm right now," said Daddy. "It happens when there's lots of snowflakes all falling at the same time. It's just like a rainstorm, but the water is frozen into snowflakes."

Daddy pointed at the computer screen next to the steering wheel. The blue dot on the map was their truck. It was surrounded by a cloud with lots of snowflakes.

Cane got scared and lay down on his seat.

"This is a big snowstorm," said Daddy. "But don't be scared. We just need to slow down, look directly ahead, and be calm."

Cane trusted his daddy, but he was still scared.

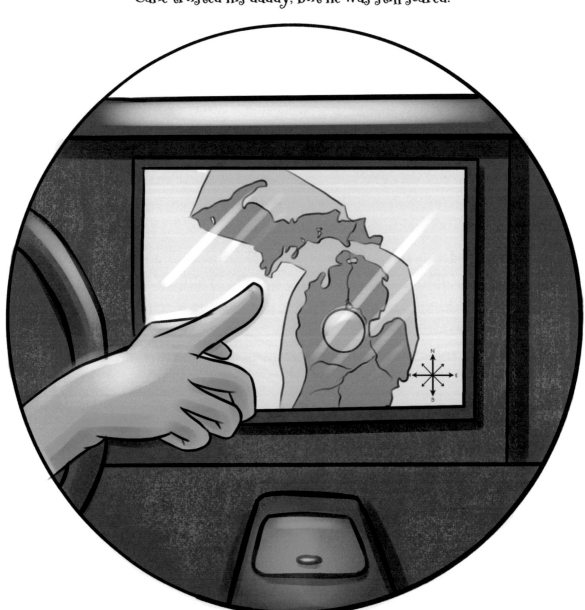

Just then, an alarm on the computer sounded, and the screen started flashing red. A loud voice from the computer scared Cane even more.

"ATTENTION. ATTENTION," the loud voice blared. "A BLIZZARD ALERT HAS BEEN ISSUED FOR WHERE YOU ARE LOCATED. IF YOU ARE TRAVELING, BE PREPARED TO TAKE SHELTER!"

Cane was very scared now. He was shaking.

Daddy reached over and petted him to try and calm him down.

"Cane, don't be scared. When there are lots of snowflakes and the wind is blowing, it creates a powerful storm called a blizzard," said Daddy.

"A blizzard can be very dangerous if you are outside or driving," Daddy explained. "You must stay inside your home or find a shelter. The wind and snowflakes make it difficult to see. We're lucky we have this special computer to help us see in the storm. Don't worry. We will be safe because we are almost at Grandma's house."

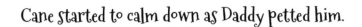

Cane started to calm down as Daddy petted him.

When Cane looked out the window, he saw fewer snowflakes and could see the trees again.

The red light on the computer screen stopped flashing, and the alarm stopped blaring. Cane could see the blue dot on the screen, and there was no more snow cloud around it. This helped him relax.

"See, Cane, the storm has passed," said Daddy. "We made it through okay. And guess what?" Daddy asked Cane.

"What, Daddy?" Cane barked.

"We're here!" Daddy exclaimed.

Cane looked out the window, and he was excited.
They had arrived at
Grandma Cindy's house.

Grandma Cindy walked out of the house and waved at Cane and Daddy as the truck was parked in the driveway.

Daddy reached over and opened the door next to Cane so that he could get out of the truck. As soon as the door opened, Cane jumped out and ran over to his grandma.

He was very happy to see her. She picked him up, hugged him tightly, and gave him a big kiss on the top of his head.

Daddy walked over and hugged both of them.

"I'm so glad you are both here for Christmas," Grandma Cindy said. "You just made it in time for Christmas Eve."

As Daddy and Cane got their bags out of the truck, they heard someone yelling.

"Merry Christmas, Cane!" yelled a man walking toward them.

It was Alejandro, Grandma's neighbor. He would babysit Cane when Daddy and Grandma were on vacation.

"I'm excited to see you, Cane," said Alejandro as he patted Cane on the head.

"I've missed you too," barked Cane.

"We arrived just in time," Daddy told Alejandro. "There is a very strong blizzard on the way. We all need to get prepared."

"Daddy says we all need to stay home and remain calm," barked Cane.

"I will go home and get ready right now," said Alejandro. "I will see you later for Christmas Eve dinner. I have made a special dessert."

"Yummy," barked Cane.

"We'll see you in a few hours," Grandma said as Alejandro walked back to his house. "We should go inside because it's cold, and it will start snowing soon."

Grandma started a fire in the fireplace. She put Cane's special bed on the ground next to the fire. He was excited to rest in his bed. The fire made him feel nice and warm since it was so cold outside.

The entire house was decorated for Christmas. Grandma's Christmas tree was next to the fireplace. It had lots of red, blue, and yellow bulbs. The lights on the tree flashed. It was very pretty.

Cane was already starting to feel the Christmas spirit, but he was also tired after the long drive and the scary blizzard, so he decided to take a nap next to the fireplace and Christmas tree.

When Cane woke up, he started to stretch his legs. Then his nose started to twitch. Something smelled very good.

He jumped out of his bed and ran to the kitchen.

Grandma was taking a tray out of the oven. He couldn't see what was on it, but whatever it was, it smelled great.

"I made some special treats for my special granddog," said Grandma.

Grandma handed Cane a Christmas cookie shaped like a candy cane.

"These are my special candy cane cookies just for you, Cane," said Grandma.

Cane took a bite of the cookie. It was warm and crispy. It tasted very good.

He jumped up and hugged Grandma to thank her for the cookie.

"Cane, let's pack up some of these cookies and take them to visit your friends," said Grandma.

Cane was very excited. He had missed his friends because he had not seen them since last summer.

Cane and Grandma walked slowly through the snow in her backyard. He could see the trees of the forest directly ahead of him. He was so excited, he started barking.

"Hey, everybody! It's me—Cane. I'm back to visit," he barked.

One by one, all of his friends started running and flying out of the forest to see him.

Brian the Black Bear was the first one to push his way through the trees. He was very large and strong.

"Cane, it's great to see you again," roared Brian.

Brenda the Beaver and Rachel the Raccoon rushed out of the woods just behind Brian the Black Bear.

"You're finally here," said Brenda the Beaver.

"Grandma Cindy said you were coming to visit, and we've been excited to see you," Rachel the Raccoon squeaked as she scampered toward Cane.

There was a large cracking noise behind them as an old tree fell down. It was his friend Dave the White-Tailed Deer. His big antlers had pushed the tree over.

"Cane, we've missed you," bellowed Dave.

"Yes, it's been too long," screeched Olivia the Snowy Owl as she circled above Cane's head.

All of the friends hugged and were happy to be together.

"Cane and I brought you some special Christmas cookies," said Grandma as she gave each of the friends a treat. "Cane, you can stay out and play with your friends for a while, but make sure you come home before it gets dark," Grandma said as she turned and started walking toward the house.

"I promise I'll be home in time for Christmas Eve dinner," barked Cane.

He turned to his friends and yelled, "Let's go!"

Cane and all of his friends ran back into the woods to start playing.

The friends arrived at their animal neighborhood. It was a big opening in the woods surrounded by trees. Along one side, there was a little stream. It was so cold, though, that all of the water was frozen into a sheet of ice.

This is where they had all built their homes.

On one side, there was a large cave opening surrounded by rocks. It was big because both Brian the Black Bear and Dave the White-Tailed Deer lived in it as roommates.

There was also a big dome made out of sticks where Brenda the Beaver and Rachel the Raccoon lived.

And above both houses was Olivia's nest. It was high up in the branches of the largest tree in the forest.

"Welcome to our homes," roared Brian.

In the center of the clearing, the animals had decorated their own Christmas tree. On it hung lots of red berries, colorful feathers, and strings of seeds. It was a beautiful tree.

"Grandma Cindy told us about her Christmas tree, so we decided to make our own," squeaked Rachel the Raccoon.

"It looks beautiful," barked Cane.

"Your grandma told us all about Christmas, the Christmas tree, and Santa Claus," bellowed Dave the White-Tailed Deer.

Cane and all the animals sat down around the Christmas tree.
"She said if we are very good boys and girls, then Santa will bring us some presents," screeched Olivia, who was sitting on a branch of the Christmas tree.

"That's how it works. If you're bad, Santa doesn't leave you any presents," barked Cane. "So it's important to be good all year. You have to mind your parents, play nice with your friends, and help people in trouble."

All the animals were excited because they'd been good all year, and it was finally Christmas Eve. Santa would arrive soon.

Brenda the Beaver started to pound the ground with her big tail.

"Hey, everybody, it's getting dark. We need to eat our dinner and get ready for bed, or Santa won't stop and leave us any presents!" Brenda yelled.

It was time for Cane to head home, or he would be late for Christmas Eve dinner. All the friends stood up and gave each other big hugs.

"Merry Christmas, everyone," Cane barked as he started running out of the clearing and into the woods on his way home to Grandma's house. "I'll come and visit you tomorrow for Christmas Day!"

"Merry Christmas!" all the friends yelled to Cane as he disappeared into the forest.

Cane arrived at Grandma's house just in time for dinner.

Grandma had cooked a big meal. There were potatoes, carrots, and roast beef.

"Cane, I cooked you a special Christmas Eve meal," Grandma said as she filled his dish with lots of food that smelled really great.

"And I made a special chocolate cake for dessert," said Alejandro, "but you have to eat all your other food first."

As everyone started eating, Cane looked out the window. He quickly became upset.

"Daddy, all the snowflakes are back," barked Cane.

Daddy walked over to the window and looked outside. There were lots of snowflakes falling, and the wind was getting stronger.

DING-DING-DING-DING!

The alarm on Daddy's computer started blaring again.

"ATTENTION. ATTENTION," the loud voice blurted. "A BLIZZARD WARNING HAS BEEN ISSUED FOR WHERE YOU LIVE. TAKE SHELTER NOW! DO NOT GO OUTSIDE. DO NOT TRAVEL!"

Cane was very scared. He ran over and jumped into Grandma's lap. She hugged him tight and started to pet him to calm him down.

"Are my friends going to be okay out in the woods?" barked Cane.

"Yes, they will be fine. They have very strong houses to keep them safe," said Grandma.

As the snow started falling harder outside, Alejandro put on his coat to leave.

"I am going home before it's too difficult to walk through the snow and the wind," said Alejandro as he waved goodbye and walked out the door.

"Be safe," barked Cane.

"This storm is going to last all night and will be very powerful," said Daddy.

"Is Santa going to be okay?" barked Cane.

Daddy petted Cane on the head.

"Santa will be fine. He and his reindeer know how to fly through the snow," said Daddy.

Daddy turned on the television and started working on his computer.
Cane watched as he checked all the weather maps. The storm was getting
bigger. It covered Grandma's entire city.

"How bad will this blizzard get tonight?" barked Cane.

DING! DING!

DING! DING!

The alarm on Daddy's computer started blaring again.

"ATTENTION. ATTENTION," the loud voice blurted. "BLIZZARD WARNING. THIS WILL BE A HISTORIC BLIZZARD. THE STRONG WINDS WILL CAUSE DAMAGE. THE ELECTRICITY WILL GO OUT. NO ONE SHOULD BE TRAVELING. STAY HOME."

Daddy started petting Cane again.

"Remember, Cane, you have to stay calm," said Daddy. "The only person traveling tonight is Santa."

"Santa and his magical reindeer and sleigh are the only ones who can safely travel in this Christmas blizzard," said Grandma.

Cane knew they were safe in their house, but now he was worried about his friends and Santa.

Daddy was also worried.

"We're going to get more than a foot of snow," said Daddy, "and the winds will be very strong. They will knock out the electricity in the house."

Grandma went to a closet and brought out some flashlights. She gave one to Daddy and put one next to Cane's bed.

"There's nothing we can do now," said Grandma. "We should all get some sleep because we'll have to shovel a lot of snow out of the driveway tomorrow."

Grandma hugged and kissed Daddy and Cane. Then she went to her
bedroom to go to sleep.

Daddy sat on the couch and checked his computer for a long time.

It was very dark outside. The snow was hitting the windows, and the wind
was loudly howling as it rushed around the house.

"Cane, don't worry about the storm. We should go to bed. Merry
Christmas," Daddy said as he hugged Cane and headed to his bedroom.

Cane crawled into his bed and fell asleep.

BANG! BANG! BANG!

The loud noise startled Cane. He quickly jumped out of his bed. It was very dark. The electricity had gone out. Some light from the fireplace was the only way he could see across the room.

BANG! BANG! BANG!

The noise was coming from the back door. Cane ran through the house to see what was making the noise. All he could hear was the wind outside. It was so dark, he couldn't see anything.

Cane jumped up and pulled on the door handle. The door opened just a crack.

WHOOSH!

The wind whipped in through the open door. It blew snow into Grandma's house.

He squinted his eyes to look outside. At first, he couldn't see anything, but then he heard a voice yelling over the noise of the wind.

"HELP!!! Cane, we need help!" bellowed Dave the White-Tailed Deer. "There's been an accident. Please come help!"

Cane was very worried. He remembered what Daddy had said—he must stay calm.

"Let me grab my flashlight. I'll be right back," barked Cane.

Cane rushed back into the house. He got the flashlight Grandma left for him, and he quickly ran back to the door.

"Jump on my back," said Dave the White-Tailed Deer. "The snow is too deep for you to walk through."

Cane jumped on Dave's back and wrapped his legs around his neck. Dave started running through the snow as quickly as he could. Cane turned on the flashlight, so Dave could see where he was going.

The blizzard's winds were blowing the snow everywhere. Neither Dave the White-Tailed Deer nor Cane could see where they were going.

Dave had to slow down when he got into the woods because the snow was too deep to run through.

As they made their way toward the animal neighborhood, Cane could barely hear his friends' voices yelling for help because the wind was so loud.

"We're coming!" bellowed Dave the White-Tailed Deer.

Cane's flashlight moved back and forth and, finally, he was able to see Brian the Black Bear surrounded by a whirl of snowflakes.

"Cane and Dave, I'm glad you made it back! The storm is getting worse!" roared Brian.

"What happened?" Cane barked. "Is everyone okay?"

"There was a big crashing noise in the woods just outside our neighborhood," squealed Rachel the Raccoon.

"We don't know what it is, but someone needs help!" yelled Brenda the Beaver.

All the friends ran into Brian and Dave's cave to get out of the blizzard's snow and wind.

"I tried to fly in the storm to see what had happened, but the wind was too strong, and I almost crashed into a tree," screeched Olivia the Snowy Owl.

WHOOSH!

The blizzard's winds whipped through the cave. It blew a lot of snow at Cane and his friends.

"Daddy says we need to stay calm and make a plan," barked Cane.

"I have really good eyesight even in the snow," screeched Olivia the Snowy Owl.

"Dave and I are big enough to walk through the snow," roared Brian the Black Bear.

"We should all go together," barked Cane. "Dave should be in the front with Brian following him. Olivia and I will ride on Dave's back, Rachel and Brenda, you should ride on Brian's back, Everyone ready?" barked Cane.

"Let's go!" all the animals yelled.

Dave the White-Tailed Deer and Brian the Black Bear slowly walked through the snow with the other animals riding on their backs.

The wind was pushing them, and the snow was starting to coat their fur and feathers.

Cane used his flashlight to help lead the way, but the snow was too thick to see anything.

And then, just over the roar of the wind, they all heard a faint voice.

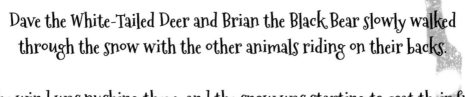

"He's over there behind those trees," screeched Olivia the Snowy Owl. "I can see his sleigh. It's turned upside down."

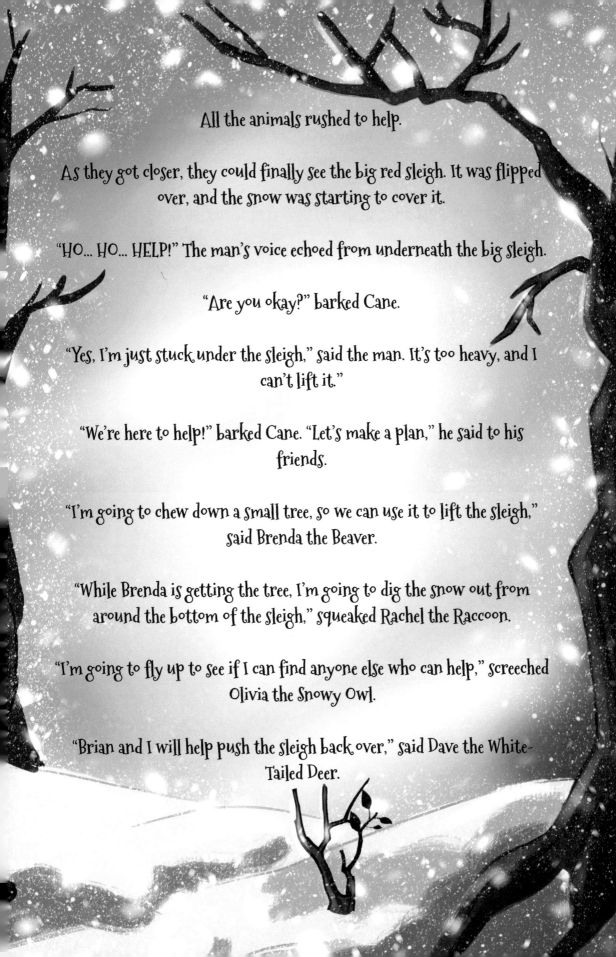

All the animals rushed to help.

As they got closer, they could finally see the big red sleigh. It was flipped over, and the snow was starting to cover it.

"HO... HO... HELP!" The man's voice echoed from underneath the big sleigh.

"Are you okay?" barked Cane.

"Yes, I'm just stuck under the sleigh," said the man. It's too heavy, and I can't lift it."

"We're here to help!" barked Cane. "Let's make a plan," he said to his friends.

"I'm going to chew down a small tree, so we can use it to lift the sleigh," said Brenda the Beaver.

"While Brenda is getting the tree, I'm going to dig the snow out from around the bottom of the sleigh," squeaked Rachel the Raccoon.

"I'm going to fly up to see if I can find anyone else who can help," screeched Olivia the Snowy Owl.

"Brian and I will help push the sleigh back over," said Dave the White-Tailed Deer.

The animals were ready. They pushed the tree under the sleigh. Cane, Brenda the Beaver, and Rachel the Raccoon started pulling on the tree. Dave the White-Tailed Deer and Brian the Black Bear started pushing on the sleigh.

It started to slowly lift off of the ground.

"Push harder!" barked Cane. "We've almost got it."

A hand in a black glove slipped out from underneath the sleigh. Then another gloved hand came out. The man used his hands to grab onto the sleigh and help lift it.

"Push!" barked Cane.

They pushed with all their might, and the sleigh flipped back over.

All the animals fell to the ground. They were exhausted.

As they sat on the ground, they stared at the man as he stood up.

He was short. He had a big white beard. He was dressed in all red from his head to his feet.

The friends couldn't believe their eyes.

They all yelled at the same time, "It's Santa Claus!"

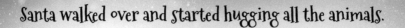

Santa walked over and started hugging all the animals.

He hugged Brenda the Beaver. He hugged Rachel the Raccoon. Santa hugged Brian the Black Bear. He wrapped his arms around Dave the White-Tailed Deer's neck. Finally, he picked up Cane and gave him a big hug and kiss on the head.

"All you animals saved me," said Santa. "I've never seen such brave animals in all my life. You stayed calm. You made a plan, and you worked together. What a great job!"

"We're just glad you are okay," barked Cane. "What happened?"

Santa told the animals about his accident. He and his reindeer were trying to fly through the blizzard, but the winds were too strong. The reins holding his reindeer snapped, and his sleigh fell into the woods. His reindeer kept flying because they couldn't land and help him.

Just then, a voice appeared from above.

"I found them! I found them!" screeched Olivia the Snowy Owl.

She landed on the corner of the sleigh and couldn't believe her eyes. Santa was standing there.

"I found your reindeer, Santa!" screeched Olivia.

"Good job, little owl," said Santa.

"But they are too afraid to land here during the blizzard," screeched Olivia.

"It seems like it's time for a new plan," barked Cane.

"Why don't we pull Santa's sleigh back to the animal neighborhood?" bellowed Dave the White-Tailed Deer.

"That's a great idea," screeched Olivia the Snowy Owl. "There's more room there for the reindeer to land."

"But how are we going to pull it?" asked Santa.

"Rachel and I will go and get some dried-out vines off the trees," said Brenda the Beaver.

"Brian and I will pull the sleigh while Santa and the other animals steer," roared Brian the Black Bear.

The vines were tied around the chests of Brian the Black Bear and Dave the White-Tailed Deer. The other animals and Santa quickly got in the sleigh.

"Here we go, everyone!" yelled Santa.

Olivia flew ahead of the team so she could tell them which way to go.

"Turn to the left around the tree, and then go straight," Olivia screeched as the sleigh slowly made its way through the forest.

Santa's sleigh moved around trees and rolled over snow-covered logs.

"We're almost there!" screeched Olivia.

Santa's sleigh finally arrived in the animal neighborhood.

Dave and Brian pulled it to the center of the clearing next to the big Christmas tree.

"That's a beautiful Christmas tree," said Santa. "You have a wonderful neighborhood, and it is full of very good boys and girls."

Santa hugged everyone again for helping save his sleigh.

"Olivia, would you fly up and tell the reindeer it's safe to land here?" asked Santa.

"I'm on my way," screeched Olivia.

WHOOSH! WHOOSH!

A noise louder than the wind swirled above their heads.

"Stand back, everyone! Here they come!" yelled Santa.

Olivia flew through the neighborhood opening and landed in the Christmas tree.

WHOOSH!!

The sound grew louder. The animals watched as eight very large flying reindeer landed in their neighborhood.

Santa walked over and hugged each of his reindeer.

"I'm glad you are all safe, but we are running out of time," said Santa.

We have to deliver presents to boys and girls all around the world.

"The blizzard has ended, so it's safe for you to fly now," barked Cane.

Santa hooked his reindeer back up to the front of his sleigh. Before he got in, he walked back over to talk to his animal friends.

"I am very proud of all of you," Santa said to the animals. "You saved my reindeer. You saved my sleigh. You saved me, and you saved Christmas."

Cane and all his friends cheered.

"It is time for me to go, and it is time for all of you to go to sleep because I can't leave any presents if you are awake," said Santa as he winked at the animals.

He jumped into his sleigh and pulled on his reindeers' reins. They ran across the clearing and just before they got to the trees, they leapt into the air and flew away pulling Santa's sleigh.

"Merry Christmas my friends!" Santa yelled as he flew out of sight.

"Merry Christmas, Santa!" all the animals yelled back.

The animals quickly said good night and headed to bed. Cane knew he had to get home quickly. He started running through the forest toward Grandma's house. The blizzard winds had stopped, but the snow on the ground was very deep.

He could see a light in the distance and heard a voice yelling, "Cane, where are you?"

"I'm right here!" barked Cane.

Cane ran toward the light. It was his daddy using a flashlight because all the lights in the house were off.

He jumped into the air, and his Daddy caught him. Daddy hugged Cane and gave him a kiss on the head.

"Grandma and I have been worried about you," said Daddy.

"I'm sorry, but my friends and I had to save Santa from the blizzard," barked Cane.

"Santa?" asked Daddy. "I can't wait to hear the story, but, you will need to tell me tomorrow. You need to go to bed."

Daddy carried Cane into the living room and put him in
his bed next to the fireplace. The fire felt nice and helped
warm Cane up.

"You need to go to sleep, Cane, or else your friend Santa
will not be able to deliver any presents," said Daddy.

"Good night, and Merry Christmas, Daddy," barked Cane.

Cane lay his head down and fell asleep in
his warm bed.

The next morning, Cane slowly woke up in his bed. He looked around the room and saw a huge pile of presents under the Christmas tree.

"Merry Christmas, Cane!" yelled Grandma.

Grandma, Daddy, and Alejandro were sitting on the couch waiting for Cane to wake up.

"Santa left lots of extra presents for you," said Daddy. "Maybe you really did save Santa last night."

"We did save him," barked Cane. "My friends and I found him trapped in the woods. We got him back in his sleigh with his reindeer just in time for him to deliver all his presents around the world."

Grandma, Daddy, Alejandro, and Cane started opening their presents.

Santa left Cane a special gift. It was a small red box with a gold bow. The tag on the present read: To the Dog That Saved Christmas, From Santa.

Cane was very excited when he opened the box. It was a brand-new red collar with a gold candy cane hanging on it. Cane's name was written in big letters on the candy cane.

"That's a very nice collar," said Daddy.

"It's from Santa. It's my new Christmas collar."

After they were done opening presents, Cane, Daddy, Alejandro, and Grandma all went to visit Cane's friends.

They trudged through the deep snow in the forest. Daddy was carrying a lot of presents. Grandma had a plate of cookies, and Alejandro was carrying a big chocolate cake.

Cane was leading the way.

They were going to surprise Cane's animal friends for Christmas.

"We're almost there," barked Cane. "They are going to be excited to see you."

When they arrived in the animal neighborhood, all of Cane's friends were sitting next to their Christmas tree opening presents.

"Merry Christmas," barked Cane.

Cane's friends were surprised by their Christmas guests. Grandma, Alejandro, and Daddy hugged all of the animals and wished them a Merry Christmas.

"Did Santa leave you presents too?" asked Cane.

"He sure did," roared Brian the Black Bear. "When we woke up, there were piles of presents for all of us under our Christmas tree."

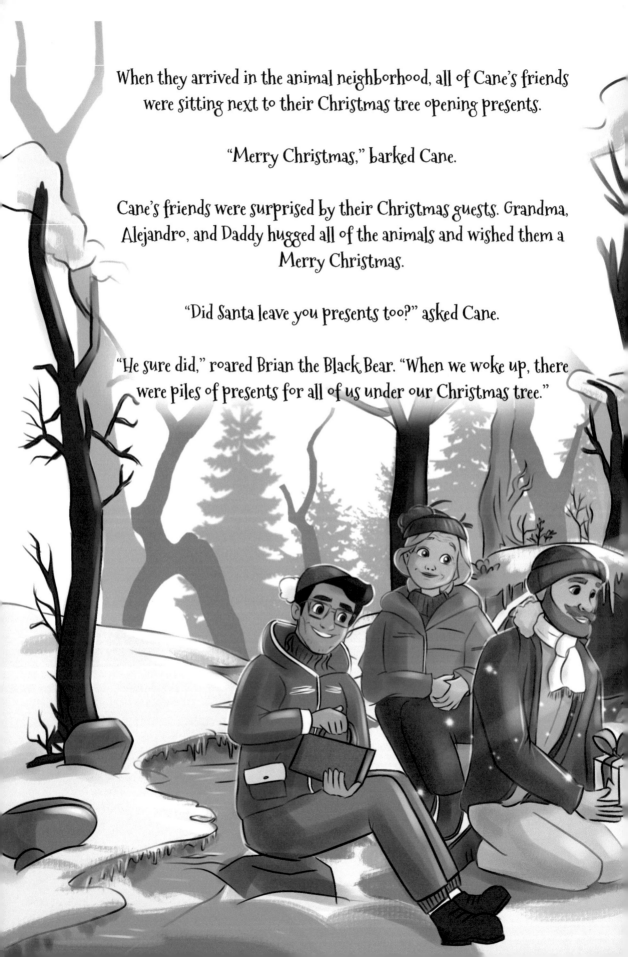

"Santa is very proud of all of you," said Daddy. "You did a great job making a plan and staying calm."

Everyone sat down next to the Christmas tree as Grandma handed out her special candy cane cookies. Cane looked around at his friends and family. It was the best Christmas he'd ever had. He was excited about the presents he had received from Santa, but he was more excited to spend time with his friends, Grandma, Daddy, and Alejandro.

"Merry Christmas, everyone," barked Cane.

"Merry Christmas!" everyone yelled.

Cane's Weather Words:

Blizzard
Cold
Freeze
Frost
Icicle
Sleet
Snow
Snowfall
Snowflake
Temperature
Wind
Winter

About Cane the Weather Dog:

Cane the Weather Dog and his daddy travel the country chasing storms and protecting people from harm. Cane has learned lots of important information about powerful storms. Along the way, he has made lots of special animal friends. Cane makes sure all his friends stay safe during bad storms.

About Daddy:

Daddy Scott is a meteorologist and environmental scientist. Every weekday morning, as a national television morning show meteorologist, he ensures Americans are prepared for the severe weather they face.

For more than a decade, Scott has been on the ground covering every major natural disaster impacting the lives of Americans. He's reported on hurricanes, floods, wildfires, tornadoes, and droughts.

Made in the USA
Columbia, SC
12 November 2024

45903777R00042